THE TINY BOOK OF
TINY HOUSES

LESTER WALKER

The Overlook Press
Woodstock, New York

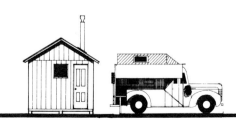

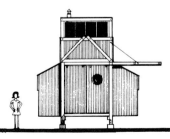

First published in 1993 by
The Overlook Press
Lewis Hollow Road
Woodstock, New York 12498

Library of Congress Cataloging-in-Publication Data

Walker, Les.
Tiny Houses
1. Small houses - United States - Designs and plans -
Amateurs' manuals. 2. Architecture, Domestic - United States
- Designs and Plans - Amateurs' manuals   I. Title.
NA7205.W36 1987 728.3'7'0222 86-21736
ISBN: 0-87951-271-7 (full-length edition)

ISBN: 0-87951-510-4

If you like *The Tiny Book of Tiny Houses,*
a full sized edition - the original *Tiny Houses-*
is available from the Overlook Press.

Printed in Mexico

Second Printing

To my wife Karen and my sons Jess and Andrew

CONTENTS

INTRODUCTION

This book began four years ago as a pattern book illustrating several tiny houses as affordable build-it-yourself vacation homes. The idea was to provide the reader with plans for very, very inexpensive small dwelling projects that would take a week to two to build. My goal was to inspire people of all ages and degrees of carpentry skill who previously could not afford a second home to take hammer in hand and build themselves a little dream. It seems to me that one of the great thrills in life is to inhabit a building that one has built oneself.

Ever since the first manned space capsule was sent into orbit in 1961 I have been interested in perfectly designed tiny living spaces. I kept careful notes on projects that I liked and began gathering plans for houses with under three hundred square feet of space that might easily be detailed and described. A few years ago I contacted Michael Jantzen, Jeff Milstein, Allan Wexler, and Mary Carrabba, and they agreed to allow me to include their work. I challenged my City College architecture students to design a tiny house of their own, and some of those were to be included here. The book took shape. I would include about twenty tiny houses with schematic plans showing how they could be constructed. Just when I had collected a nice list of tiny houses and had begun laying out the book, the idea began to change. First, practically every conversation I entered that began with "What are you doing lately?" ended in a discussion of some incredible tiny house that I hadn't considered. I particularly remember three years ago in Reston, Virginia, speaking with a group of people who had assembled to celebrate the opening of *House Beautiful* magazine's "Best Small House '84," a national house design competition that I had won. After someone asked me "What's next?" the representative of the American Wood Council, sponsors of the competition, editors of two local newspapers, a *House Beautiful* editor and a Reston advertising executive and his wife became absorbed in the idea of tiny houses. I learned about Thoreau's cabin, the Martha's Vineyard Campground cottages, and the tiny writer's huts in which Hollywood movie scriptwriters in 1930s were forced to stay until they completed their jobs. I also learned to bring up the tiny-house subject whenever I could, because it seemed like everyone had a favorite that could take me on a tiny house-hunting adventure.

Second, I found that as I laid out the book I was spending more time and space showing how to build the house than how it looked, how it came to be, or how it felt to be inside. I found that I was borrowing too much from books that explained building methods much better than I could.

I decided then that I could best serve the reader by providing more inspirational information, such as pictures of the buildings, drawings of interior furniture layouts, construction sequences showing how easy it is, and the story of the house. I included the basic architectural drawings of elevations and plans, having concluded that once the reader chose a house, he or she could use these drawings together with a housebuilding guide to build his or her tiny house.

Notes about the Houses:

The first tiny house I remember seeing and categorizing as a tiny, tiny house was a complete surprise. In the summer of 1963,

I discovered one while hiking along what seemed to me to be a very treacherous untraveled animal trail on a remote part of Maine's coastline, about an hour east of Cutler. I couldn't imagine how anyone might have transported materials to this spot without having lugged them over windswept cliffs and slippery rocks. But there it was, a tiny little gable-roofed cabin no larger than 8′ × 10′ built entirely of tarpaper and driftwood, complete with an Adirondack style built-in twig bed, a perfect little kitchen that used water form a nearby spring, and a writing desk under a window facing the sea. Set back about one hundred feet from the ocean on a rocky beach in a small cove, the house was surrounded by cliffs topped with huge hemlock and pine trees.

Later, when I got back to town and learned that it was built by a little lady in her eighties who loved nature and solitude, I realized that the art of building was not necessarily reserved for architects and builders. All that was needed, it seemed, was the will. Two years ago, I hiked back to this site with my camera, notepad, and the hope that I could find this little building . No luck. A big storm had apparently blown it away. But this home will remain in my mind as one of the most beautiful buildings I've ever seen. It may have been the inspiration for this book.

My early research was done primarily by mail or phone. For example, one day a photograph of a tiny house appeared in my mail accompanied by a letter from my aunt and uncle who had just visited the Carmel Bay area in California and had photographed one of many tiny houses in a community there. When I asked them where it was they could only provide me with the name of the motel where they had stayed. I wrote the motel and asked them to slip a letter under the door of the tiny house, enclosing the photograph so the motel might find it. Miraculously, I received a return letter from the owners of the Pink House including a bit of history and some sketched floor plans. My detective work had paid off.

Later, as I began to need more information about the houses, I planned visits to draw and discuss them in person. One of my more recent tiny house-hunting adventures happened last winter on a quest to photograph ice fishing shanties in Upstate New York. As I walked over the slick twenty-four-inch-thick ice of Lake Champlain I had no idea how far I was from shore: my mind was focused on the wonderful little communities of buildings— each one more exciting than the last. When I realized that it was snowing and the wind was beginning to howl, I looked for my car on shore. I couldn't see it. To add to my anxiety, I learned that I had to shuffle my feet because the fresh layer of snow made the ice much more slippery. By the time I got to my car, about two miles later, I was caked with snow, my legs were rubbery with exhaustion, and my nose was frozen. I felt like Admiral Perry in the Arctic, tracking the elusive ice fishing shanty.

Another adventure—to photograph dune shacks—took me across the great sand dunes at the tip of Cape Cod near Provincetown. I missed my contact, a ten-year-old daughter of a friend of a friend, who was to escort me to the shacks. Because my time was limited I decided to make the trip myself. I had no idea it was like the Sahara out there! My destination was only about a forty-minute walk away but the heat off the sand, the difficulty in walking, and the desolate dune landscape drained my energy and made me quite thirsty, to say the least. Luckily, a cool glass of water and a friendly face greeted me before long in the shack known as Thalasa.

Researching this book has been a wonderful experience. Almost every house seemed to begin with an idea from a book, magazine, friend, or colleague, lead to a most interesting, sometimes thrilling photography/sketching/interview session; and end with a quiet week at my graphics table synthesizing my information into drawings and pasting up camera-ready mechanical boards from which this book was printed.

Notes on Building:
There are no plans available for any of the tiny houses shown in this book. Please do not send letters asking for plans. If you choose to build one of the houses, the basic dimensions, materials, and methods are discussed, but a complete set of construction drawings was impossible to include.

Notes on the Photographs:

All of the photographs in the book are by me except those listed on page 94. These people were kind enough to share their work with me.

Notes about the Drawings:

All of the drawings were done on 100 percent rag tracing paper at $\frac{1}{8}'' = 1'0''$ scale with 4×0 and 2×0 Mars Staetler ink pens. They were reduced with photostats to 68 percent of their original size for the final graphics of the book. Because all the drawings are drawn to the same scale, they can be compared to one another throughout the book.

I am sure most people, if they so desired, could research their own list of tiny houses just as remarkable as those illustrated here. If I had written this book at a different time in my life, the houses would probably have been entirely different. Once one starts seriously observing and studying, the number of tiny houses in any given geographical area can be endless.

Finally, I'd like to express what a great expereince every aspect of this book was, from research to final artwork and editing. I have many new friends because of it and a fresh outlook on my architecture and teaching. I hope this appreciation come through, and I do hope you enjoy the book.

Lester Walker
Woodstock, New York

FRONTIER CABIN

16' × 14' plus sleeping attic
224 square feet

Among America's most interesting tiny houses from an anthro-
pological point of view are the log cabins built first by Swedish
settlers and later by frontiersmen and traders throughout the
country. The cabin shown here is a perfect one-room portrayal
of frontier living quarters built around 1800 in Grainger County,
Tennessee. Now part of the Museum of Appalachia in Norris,
Tennessee, it is known as the Arnwine Cabin, named after its
original owner, John Wesley Arnwine and his family. It is included
in the National Register of Historic Places.

All family living functions took place in the single room: living,
dining, and kitchen by day and sleeping by night. Children slept
in the attic (reachable by ladder) but spent the day in the main
room with the rest of the family. The tiny room evolved into four
separate living areas: entry (coats, boots, outdoor tools), kitchen
(fireplace, food preparation, and storage), bedroom (bed that
doubled as a couch in the day), and the entire space was used
as a "living room" when necessary.

Except for the stone fireplace, the interior was constructed from logs, hewn to perform their specific function. Log cabins built today are apt to have more windows, at least in the doors.

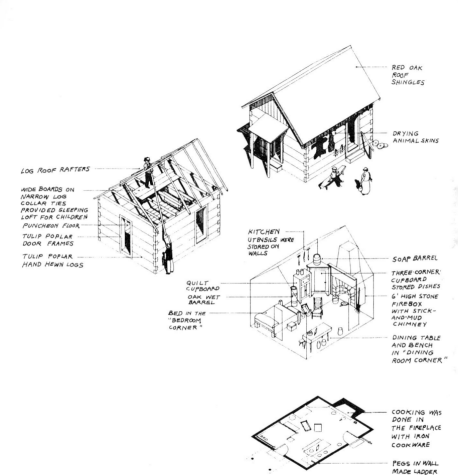

RED OAK
ROOF
SHINGLES

DRYING
ANIMAL SKINS

LOG ROOF RAFTERS

WIDE BOARDS ON
NARROW LOG
COLLAR TIES
PROVIDED SLEEPING
LOFT FOR CHILDREN

PUNCHEON FLOOR

TULIP POPLAR
DOOR FRAMES

TULIP POPLAR
HAND HEWN LOGS

KITCHEN
UTENSILS WERE
STORED ON
WALLS

SOAP BARREL

THREE-CORNER
CUPBOARD
STORED DISHES

6' HIGH STONE
FIREBOX
WITH STICK-
AND-MUD
CHIMNEY

QUILT
CUPBOARD

OAK WET
BARREL

BED IN THE
"BEDROOM
CORNER"

DINING TABLE
AND BENCH
IN "DINING
ROOM CORNER"

COOKING WAS
DONE IN
THE FIREPLACE
WITH IRON
COOKWARE

PEGS IN WALL
MADE LADDER
TO CHILDREN'S
SLEEPING
LOFT

19

CAPE COD HONEYMOON COTTAGE

18′ × 16′ plus sleeping attic
288 square feet

The quintessential in romantic tiny houses is the original honeymoon cottage version of the well-known Cape Cod house. During the eighteenth century, when young settlers were inhabiting the Cape Cod area, they built half-sized or partially built Cape Cod houses and added to them as their families grew and their wealth increased.

The original design was a simple gable-roofed structure built with an oversized frame on huge 10″ × 10″ oak sills. As the dunes shifted, ship's carpenters used teams of horses to drag the houses across the sand to more desirable sites. Eighteen-inch-wide vertical planks provided an ingenious means of both stabilizing the post-and-beam frame and of sheathing the native cedar shingles on the outside and plaster on the inside. The outside of the Cape Cod has no projections or extraneous decoration that might prove vulnerable to ocean gale-force winds.

Inside, the rooms were clustered around a large brick chimney that opened into a fireplace used for cooking, heating, and light.

The attic was partitioned into small bedrooms with windows in the gable end of the building.

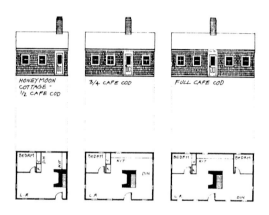

HONEY MOON COTTAGE - ½ CAPE COD

3/4 CAPE COD

FULL CAPE COD

The Cape Cod was originally a fisherman's cottage, built in the vernacular style, with local materials allowed to weather. During the 1940s and 1950s and 1960s it was extremely popular with the prefabricating home industry because of its simple shape and romantic past. The most commonly built house in America, the Cape Cod makes for a perfect tiny vacation home or honeymoon cottage.

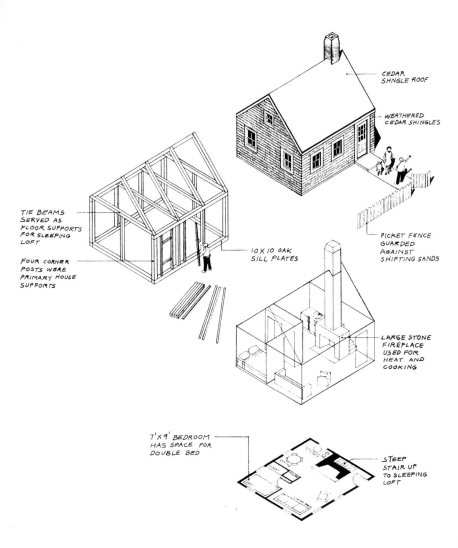

CEDAR SHNGLE ROOF

WEATHERED CEDAR SHINGLES

PICKET FENCE GUARDED AGAINST SHIFTING SANDS

TIE BEAMS SERVED AS FLOOR SUPPORTS FOR SLEEPING LOFT

FOUR CORNER POSTS WERE PRIMARY HOUSE SUPPORTS

10 X 10 OAK SILL PLATES

LARGE STONE FIREPLACE USED FOR HEAT AND COOKING

7' X 9' BEDROOM HAS SPACE FOR DOUBLE BED

STEEP STAIR UP TO SLEEPING LOFT

23

HENRY THOREAU'S CABIN

15′ × 10′ plus root cellar and attic
150 square feet

Beginning in late March of 1845, Henry David Thoreau built a tiny house on the shore of Walden Pond in Concord, Massachusetts, at a cost of $28.12½. He spent two years in this cabin, built with his own hands, while proving his famous experiment—that man could live happily and independently of other men. In his book *Walden*, Thoreau left a complete description of his house (including a materials list, dimensions, building techniques, and cost) that has enabled the reconstruction of many exact replicas by Thoreau admirers.

The most interesting aspect of the Thoreau Cabin is the frame. Thoreau economized on the work required to build a squared frame by hewing only the necessary edges of each frame member.

"Near the end of March, 1845, I borrowed an axe and went down to the woods by Walden Pond, nearest to where I intended to build my house, and began to cut down some tall, arrowy white pines, still in their youth, for timber."

"So I went on for some days cutting and hewing timber, and also studding rafters."

"I hewed the main timbers six inches square, most of the studs on two sides only, and the rafters and floor timbers on one side, leaving the rest of the bark on, so that they were just as straight and much stronger than sawed ones. Each stick was carefully mortised and tenoned by its stump, for I had borrowed other tools by this time."

"By the middle of April, for I had made no haste in my work, but rather made the most of it, my house was framed and ready for the raising."

Thoreau moved into his house on the Fourth of July, 1845, but continued to work on it as time permitted.

"I built the chimney after my hoeing in the fall, before a fire became necessary for warmth, doing my cooking in the meanwhile out of doors on the ground, early in the morning."

—quotes from *Walden*

Thoreau finally completed his house by plastering the interior on November 12, 1845.

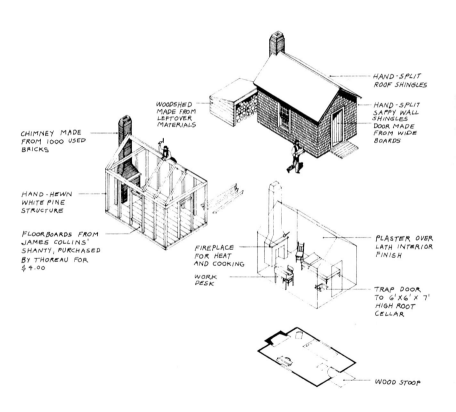

HAND-SPLIT ROOF SHINGLES

HAND-SPLIT SAPPY WALL SHINGLES

DOOR MADE FROM WIDE BOARDS

WOODSHED MADE FROM LEFTOVER MATERIALS

CHIMNEY MADE FROM 1000 USED BRICKS

HAND-HEWN WHITE PINE STRUCTURE

FLOORBOARDS FROM JAMES COLLINS' SHANTY, PURCHASED BY THOREAU FOR $4.00

FIREPLACE FOR HEAT AND COOKING

WORK DESK

PLASTER OVER LATH INTERIOR FINISH

TRAP DOOR TO 6' X 6' X 7' HIGH ROOT CELLAR

WOOD STOOP

CAMPGROUND COTTAGE

19'-6" × 11'-4" plus sleeping attic
221 square feet

In the mid-nineteenth century, America was dotted with Methodist camp-meeting grounds whre religious revivals, lasting several days, would occur regularly. (By 1875 there were eight permanent campgrounds spaced across Massachusetts alone.) Revivalists would arrive at one of these sites, rent a tent, dine and wash communally, and participate in religious meetings held in a clearing surrounded by tents.

The largest of these Methodist campgrounds is Wesleyan Grove in Oak Bluffs (named Cottage City until 1907), Martha's Vineyard, off the coast of Cape Cod, Massachusetts. The special resort qualities of the island and its close proximity to large urban areas caused the Wesleyan Grove campground to grow almost overnight. In 1840, eight hundred people attended weekly meetings with two thousand more arriving just for Sunday services. By 1858, over twelve thousand people were attending the Sunday meeting in what was proclaimed to be the largest camp meeting in the world. The tents had evolved into canvas-topped, wood-sided, wood-framed, candlelit structures that glowed at night,

further enhancing the religious ambiance of the community. Church correspondents called it a "celestial city."

The prototypical campground cottage plan evolved from that of the tents, with a larger room in the front, separated from a smaller room behind by a decorative arched partition. This second room contained a narrow stair that led to the upper sleeping level. Originally, kitchens and outhouses were separated from the cottages. During the early part of the twentieth century, small kitchens and bathrooms were added to the rear of the cottages but they had little effect on the livability of the plan.

By 1859, wood-sided tents had reached their peak, numbering well over four hundred. Many were quite refined and decorative in appearance and were, of course, an interesting link between the first plain canvas tents and the classic Carpenter Gothic cottages that exist today.

By 1864, forty tiny prefabricated Carpenter Gothic wooden houses had been built, sprinkled among five hundred canvas and wood-sided tents, constructed on their original tent platforms. For the next decade, every year fifteen to fifty new wooden cottages replaced the tents, each with more elaborate Carpenter Gothic ornamentation than the next. Today three hundred twenty beautifully preserved wooden cottages remain.

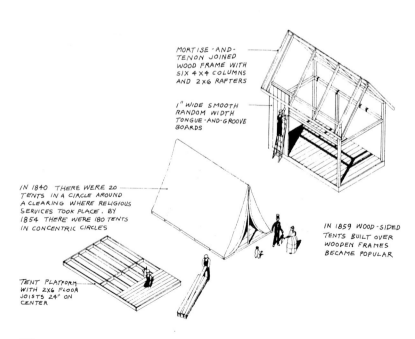

MORTISE-AND-TENON JOINED WOOD FRAME WITH SIX 4X4 COLUMNS AND 2X6 RAFTERS

1" WIDE SMOOTH RANDOM WIDTH TONGUE-AND-GROOVE BOARDS

IN 1840 THERE WERE 20 TENTS IN A CIRCLE AROUND A CLEARING WHERE RELIGIOUS SERVICES TOOK PLACE. BY 1854 THERE WERE 180 TENTS IN CONCENTRIC CIRCLES

IN 1859 WOOD-SIDED TENTS BUILT OVER WOODEN FRAMES BECAME POPULAR

TENT PLATFORM WITH 2X6 FLOOR JOISTS 24" ON CENTER

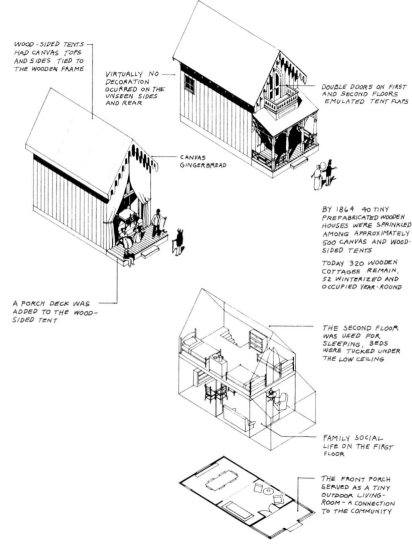

WOOD-SIDED TENTS HAD CANVAS TOPS AND SIDES TIED TO THE WOODEN FRAME

VIRTUALLY NO DECORATION OCURRED ON THE UNSEEN SIDES AND REAR

DOUBLE DOORS ON FIRST AND SECOND FLOORS EMULATED TENT FLAPS

CANVAS GINGERBREAD

A PORCH DECK WAS ADDED TO THE WOOD-SIDED TENT

BY 1864 40 TINY PREFABRICATED WOODEN HOUSES WERE SPRINKLED AMONG APPROXIMATELY 500 CANVAS AND WOOD-SIDED TENTS

TODAY 320 WOODEN COTTAGES REMAIN, 52 WINTERIZED AND OCCUPIED YEAR-ROUND

THE SECOND FLOOR WAS USED FOR SLEEPING, BEDS WERE TUCKED UNDER THE LOW CEILING

FAMILY SOCIAL LIFE ON THE FIRST FLOOR

THE FRONT PORCH SERVED AS A TINY OUTDOOR LIVING-ROOM~ A CONNECTION TO THE COMMUNITY

33

At the turn of the century, some of the campground cottages were connected together with wooden walkways—an interesting expression of community. Private second-floor cantilevered balconies were common.

Many campground cottages used the popular Carpenter Gothic board-and-batten siding to emphasize the vertical line. But many more, as pictured above, used flush vertical boards to simulate a cut-stone facade, popular with the Early Gothic Revival style.

In the 1920s and 1930s private porches were built facing the community pathway. These porches created a protected out-door living space, a king of soft buffer between the private living room and the public outdoors.

Because the cottages are often grouped closely together, most of the ornamentation is oriented toward the front, and it is there that a hundred-year "gingerbread" competition has been waged. Over forty-five different decoration patterns have been counted and, with the endless variety of window and door types, balconies, proches, shutters, and wall treatments, all using the Carpenter Gothic vocabulary, a seemingly infinite amount of delicate tiny houses has been built. Today the competition centers around color, bright, high-gloss, attention-getting colors in combinations never dreamed of: one house is two shades of day-glo pink, another is purple and white.

As one walks around this tiny colorful village on paths draped with huge elm and sycamore trees, one is struck with how perfect the place is for neighborhood living. Because the houses are little and their colors bright, there is a strong sense of community identity. Because of the tiny scale, trees seem larger, nature seems larger, the car and other machines seem out of place, and people seem very important.

SUNDAY HOUSE

14' × 14' plus sleeping attic
196 square feet

The Sunday house was built by the early rural German residents of Gillespie County in Fredericksburg, Texas, for use when they came to town to worship or to do their marketing on weekends. These tiny buildings, often no more that a 15' × 15' room with sleeping attic above, were unique to Fredericksburg, and only a few remain. A good example is the one shown here, the Weber House, located on the grounds of the Pioneer Museum on the main street of Fredericksburg.

From the 1880s through the 1920s farmers and ranchers would habitually come to town on Saturday morning to do their marketing and visiting and then went to church and Sunday school on Sunday morning, returning home that evening. The Sunday houses they built were equipped with just the essentials—beds, table and benches, a cupboard, a wood heat/cookstove, perhaps a cot, a rocking chair, and some cooking utensils. If the house was crowded, the adults ate first while the children played outside. When the men had finally taken their conversation to the front porch, the children sat

down for *zweiter Tisch*. The Weber House has an outside portable ladder to the children's sleeping attic, but many Sunday houses had outdoor stairs .

Each Sunday-house builder carefully considered his needs before he constructed his little town home. If a family lived near town and used the Sunday house only for Sunday dinner, they would build a one-room wood-frame house with a front porch. Large families who traveled fifteen or twenty miles to town in a buggy or wagon often liked the one-and-a-half-story wood-frame house with two compact first-floor rooms and a large sleeping attic above.

When, around 1920, the automobile quickened the pace of transportation, Sunday houses were no longer needed. Many became retirement homes for older farmers who chose to move into town. They often added lean-to kitchens and bathrooms. For this reason, there are very few Sunday houses left in their original condition.

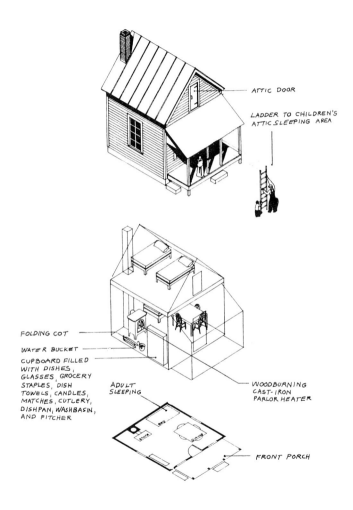

ATTIC DOOR

LADDER TO CHILDREN'S ATTIC SLEEPING AREA

FOLDING COT

WATER BUCKET

CUPBOARD FILLED WITH DISHES, GLASSES, GROCERY STAPLES, DISH TOWELS, CANDLES, MATCHES, CUTLERY, DISHPAN, WASHBASIN, AND PITCHER

ADULT SLEEPING

WOODBURNING CAST-IRON PARLOR HEATER

FRONT PORCH

43

EARTHQUAKE REFUGEE SHACK

14' × 10'
140 square feet

In 1906, after the most destructive earthquake in San Francisco history, the United States Army built 5,610 tiny redwood and fir "relief houses" as makeshift homes for twenty thousand refugees. Built with their sides practically touching, they were packed into eleven refugee camps, and rented for two dollars per month until the city was rebuilt. Designed by John McLare, the "Father of Golden Gate Park," they have been referred to as earthquake cottages, wood shanties, camp cottages, earthquake memories, unsightly wooden shacks, and "the teeniest, cutest little dovecotes of houses ever saw" (*San Francisco Chronicle*, 21 October 1906). There were four types: type "A" (140 square feet, cost $100); type "B" (252 square feet, cost $135); type "C" (375 square feet, cost $150); and type "D" (cost $741). There were five hundred type "A"'s built—the kind shown here. Kitchen and bathing facilities were communal, located outside the shacks.

Refugee shacks were built in very tight rows and painted olive drab to blend in with the greenery of the site. At one time the shacks held a population of 16,448 people.

By late 1907, many refugees had been relocated. The shacks were then carted by horse all over the city and converted into rental cottages, garages, storage spaces, or shops.

Over the years, the shacks have been all but forgotten. What cottages are left are overshadowed by modern developments,

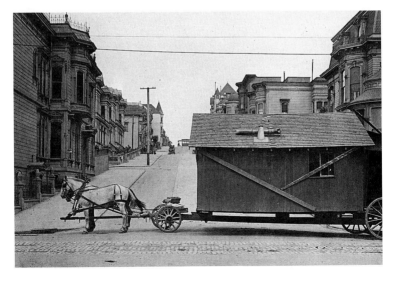

wedged between apartment buildings and condominium complexes.

The type "A" refugee shacks were remarkably well designed considering they cost only one hundred dollars. The quality of their craftsmanship and building technology was such that many have survived and are being lived in today. The Bailey Shack, owned and inhabited by Bill Bailey, is a perfect example. Located next to a huge office building on a tiny plot at the top of Telegraph Hill overlooking the city, it has to be one of San Francisco's most charming homes.

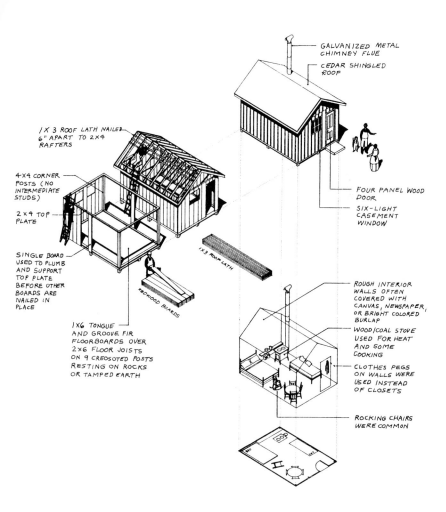

GALVANIZED METAL
CHIMNEY FLUE

CEDAR SHINGLED
ROOF

1 X 3 ROOF LATH NAILED
6" APART TO 2x4
RAFTERS

4X4 CORNER
POSTS (NO
INTERMEDIATE
STUDS)

2 X 4 TOP
PLATE

SINGLE BOARD
USED TO PLUMB
AND SUPPORT
TOP PLATE
BEFORE OTHER
BOARDS ARE
NAILED IN
PLACE

1X6 TONGUE
AND GROOVE FIR
FLOOR BOARDS OVER
2x6 FLOOR JOISTS
ON 9 CREOSOTED POSTS
RESTING ON ROCKS
OR TAMPED EARTH

1X3 ROOF LATH

REDWOOD BOARDS

FOUR PANEL WOOD
DOOR

SIX-LIGHT
CASEMENT
WINDOW

ROUGH INTERIOR
WALLS OFTEN
COVERED WITH
CANVAS, NEWSPAPER,
OR BRIGHT COLORED
BURLAP

WOOD/COAL STOVE
USED FOR HEAT
AND SOME
COOKING

CLOTHES PEGS
ON WALLS WERE
USED INSTEAD
OF CLOSETS

ROCKING CHAIRS
WERE COMMON

ROLLING HOME

7' × 6'
42 square feet

This tiny rolling home, a remodeled 1949 International delivery van named ''Patience,'' is one of many in a wonderful book called *Rolling Homes: Handmade Houses on Wheels*, by Jane Lidz. The van shown here was converted into living quarters in 1978 at the cost of $1,500. It is a complete living environment on wheels with sink, shower, toilet, lights, heat, cooking, and refrigeration. Its plush knotty-pine interior was crafted over a four-month period by a young couple interested in travel and a second home.

A rooftop, boxlike structure on the exterior of the truck is used to raisee the roof level to gain standing room (photograph at the right), and three small boxes added to the sides of the truck provide more interior work space. The inside is wonderfully handcrafted with wood paneling, carpeting, handmade quilts, secondhand windows, and a wide variety of functioning antiques, such as the wrought-iron cookstove, the porcelain sink, and several oil lamps. The ambiance is one of a cozy home—unique when it's inside a delivery van.

The water system begins with a plastic, recreation-vehicle twelve-gallon water storage tank mounted on the exterior of the truck, filled whenever possible. It is painted black so that the water retains solar heat. The water is pumped manually by a combination faucet/pump into a standard porcelain sink. This system can be designed from any recreation-vehicle accessory catalog.

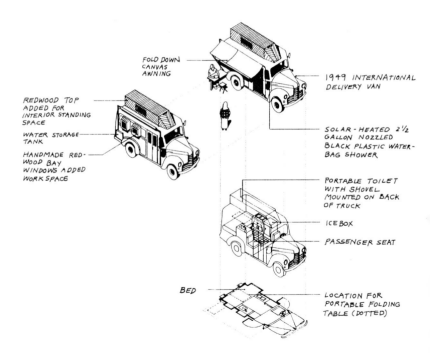

FOLD DOWN CANVAS AWNING

1949 INTERNATIONAL DELIVERY VAN

REDWOOD TOP ADDED FOR INTERIOR STANDING SPACE

WATER STORAGE TANK

HANDMADE RED-WOOD BAY WINDOWS ADDED WORK SPACE

SOLAR-HEATED 2½ GALLON NOZZLED BLACK PLASTIC WATER-BAG SHOWER

PORTABLE TOILET WITH SHOVEL MOUNTED ON BACK OF TRUCK

ICE BOX

PASSENGER SEAT

BED

LOCATION FOR PORTABLE FOLDING TABLE (DOTTED)

ICE FISHING SHANTY

7' x 4'-6"
32 square feet

Ice fishing shanties are popular forms of tiny housing in North America wherever there are frozen lakes with fish. Some states, such as Vermont and Minnesota, have wintertime lake villages of thousands of tiny utilitarian buildings, each more special than another.

The basic ice fishing shanty costs about five hundred dollars to build, seats two in a space that contains a kerosene stove, bunks for occasional overnight sleeping, a card table and shelves for food, utensils, and radio. Fishing is done by viewing outside "tip-ups": a fishing line is placed in a hole drilled in the ice and when a fish takes the bait a flag indicator is tipped up. Sometimes a line is placed directly through a removable panel in the floor of the shanty covering a drilled ice hole, a procedure used for smelt fishing.

Most ice fishing shanties are about 30 square feet and most are the same basic shape. But the materials and craftsmanship used to construct them vary widely. In a village of one

or two hundred shanties, there are always twenty or thirty that really catch the eye. These are the ones whose owners are serious do-it-yourselfers and who have set out to build themselves a little masterpiece.

Ice fishing shanty villages seem eerily deserted on cold days when everyone is inside fishing. The tiny scale of the buildings and the neatness of the folk architecture create a wonderful kind of anarchistic, unplanned community existing nowhere but on a frozen lake.

The ice fishing shanty is built on 2×6 sled runners so that it can be pulled (usually by pickup truck) onto the ice or moved to a better location. When the ice fishing season ends, they are loaded into the pickup and taken home to rest in the backyard until the next winter.

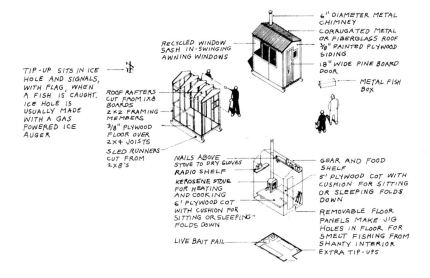

6" DIAMETER METAL CHIMNEY

CORRUGATED METAL OR FIBERGLASS ROOF

3/8" PAINTED PLYWOOD SIDING

18" WIDE PINE BOARD DOOR

METAL FISH BOX

RECYCLED WINDOW SASH IN-SWINGING AWNING WINDOWS

TIP-UP SITS IN ICE HOLE AND SIGNALS, WITH FLAG, WHEN A FISH IS CAUGHT. ICE HOLE IS USUALLY MADE WITH A GAS POWERED ICE AUGER

ROOF RAFTERS CUT FROM 1X8 BOARDS

2X2 FRAMING MEMBERS

3/8" PLYWOOD FLOOR OVER 2X4 JOISTS

SLED RUNNERS CUT FROM 2X8's

NAILS ABOVE STOVE TO DRY GLOVES

RADIO SHELF

KEROSENE STOVE FOR HEATING AND COOKING

6' PLYWOOD COT WITH CUSHION FOR SITTING OR SLEEPING FOLDS DOWN

LIVE BAIT PAIL

GEAR AND FOOD SHELF

5' PLYWOOD COT WITH CUSHION FOR SITTING OR SLEEPING FOLDS DOWN

REMOVABLE FLOOR PANELS MAKE JIG HOLES IN FLOOR FOR SMELT FISHING FROM SHANTY INTERIOR EXTRA TIP-UPS

57

BOLT-TOGETHER HOUSE

8′ × 8′ plus three 4′ × 8′ wings plus 4′ × 8′ sleeping loft
192 square feet

The Bolt-Together House is the first of two prefabricated home structures designed by Jeff Milstein for national magazines (the other is the summer house, shown on page 62). This one, designed for the March 1972 issue of *Family Circle*, was built in a Connecticut barn and trucked to its building site in Woodstock, New York, where it was erected in a month's time. The Bolt-Together House has two sleeping areas, a small kitchen and bathroom, and a living/dining space that opens to the outside by sliding open an 8′ × 8′ barn door. It was built in 1971 for $2,500 including all lumber, hardware, fixtures, appliances, woodburning stove and chimney, built-in beds and mattresses, plumbing, and electrical materials. The twenty-five thousand sets of plans sold was a *Family Circle* record.

Prefabricated, preinsulated plywood sandwich panels are made to bolt to the frame. window panels are constructed with redwood and Plexiglas and also bolt to the frame.

The frame is made from 6 × 6 columns with 2 × 6 and 2 × 4 braces painted with glossy bright enamel for definition. The panels are engineered to be bolted to the inside of the frame (exposing the frame on the exterior) so that they give rigidity to the structure.

Three 4' × 8' cruciform wings (in plan), one containing kitchen and bath, another a bed and closet, and the third the woodstove and living area, all borrow from a central 8' × 8' × 16' high volume. When it is bedtime, the volume serves the bedroom, and when it is daytime, the volumes serves the living room.

The exterior is rough-sawn, T-111 plywood, and the frame is painted, smooth structural lumber. The roof is of corrugated aluminum. Jeff Milstein grew up and was educated in California. His work is a mixture of the San Francisco Bay Region style (very rustic and, lately, affected by local vernacular barns and sheds) and the high-tech, off-the-shelf, kit-of-parts style espoused by Charles Eames of Los Angeles. The Bolt-Together House is an excellent example of both.

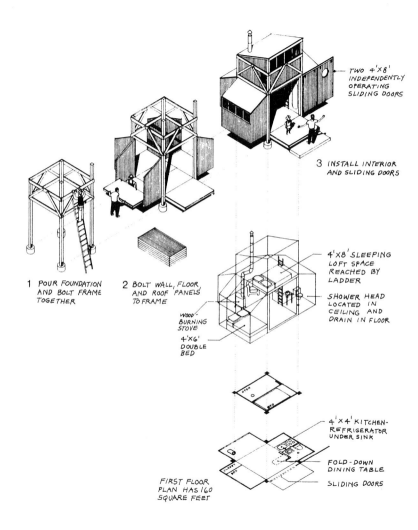

TWO 4'X8'
INDEPENDENTLY
OPERATING
SLIDING DOORS

3 INSTALL INTERIOR
AND SLIDING DOORS

1 POUR FOUNDATION
AND BOLT FRAME
TOGETHER

2 BOLT WALL, FLOOR
AND ROOF PANELS
TO FRAME

4'X8' SLEEPING
LOFT SPACE
REACHED BY
LADDER

SHOWER HEAD
LOCATED IN
CEILING AND
DRAIN IN FLOOR

WOOD-
BURNING
STOVE

4'X6'
DOUBLE
BED

4'X4' KITCHEN-
REFRIGERATOR
UNDER SINK

FOLD-DOWN
DINING TABLE

SLIDING DOORS

FIRST FLOOR
PLAN HAS 160
SQUARE FEET

61

SUMMER HOUSE

10' × 10' plus two sleeping lofts
180 square feet

This panelized summer cottage is another one of Jeff Milstein's kit-of-parts houses, this one designed in 1980 for *Family Circle* magazine as a tiny vacation house for experienced do-it-yourself builders. The house has two little 4' × 10' attic sleeping lofts, a bathroom and a kitchen sharing a tiny sink strategically placed under the ladder to the loft, and a common living/dining space with front porch.

The summer house makes an interesting comparison with the Texas Sunday House. Both have attic sleeping, both are one room in size, both have a small front porch, and both have a bit of Carpenter Gothic trim. But the summer house, while smaller, has inside bathroom and kitchen facilities. It would be interesting to bring back some of those turn-of-the century Texas churchgoers to show them the camper equipment technology that is at the heart of this tiny house.

64

As shown in the photograph on the left, prefabricated wall and roof panels are transported to the building site and erected on a 10′ × 10′ deck, which, in turn, rests on four treated posts set below the frost line. The house was designed with economy in mind. For example, the windows are made from stretched clear plastic, the wall panels from 2 × 3 studs, the siding is ½″ CDX plywood, the roof is roll roofing, and the kitchen and bathroom are designed with off-the-shelf camper equipment and hardware, requiring no plumbing or electricity.

Though compact, the large windows facing a view of the sky, and the open slot between the lofts to the roof create a spacious feeling. It can be panelized as shown or built with standard platform-frame construction methods with 2 × 3 stud walls.

The panels, illustrated below, are made with ½″ CDX plywood and 2 × 3 studs every 2′-0″ on center, and two coats of exterior paint are applied. The panels are uninsulated, but rigid insulation could be installed between the studs and another layer of protective plywood or gypsum board applied as an interior finish.

FLOOR (2) FLOOR (1) WALL (4) WALL (1) WALL (1) WALL (2) WALL (3) ROOF (4) ROOF (2) ROOF (2)

The shared kitchen/bathroom sink and camper water-supply system is beautifully designed below the ladder in a place that would normally be wasted. A small three foot by four foot room adjacent to the ladder contains a portable toilet. The drawing below shows how various catalog-ordered parts are used to create what is normally the most difficult and expensive part of any house to construct.

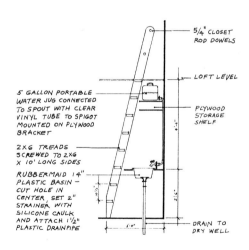

5/4" CLOSET ROD DOWELS

LOFT LEVEL

5 GALLON PORTABLE WATER JUG CONNECTED TO SPOUT WITH CLEAR VINYL TUBE TO SPIGOT MOUNTED ON PLYWOOD BRACKET

PLYWOOD STORAGE SHELF

2X6 TREADS SCREWED TO 2X6 X 10' LONG SIDES

RUBBERMAID 14" PLASTIC BASIN — CUT HOLE IN CENTER, SET 2" STRAINER WITH SILICONE CAULK AND ATTACH 1½" PLASTIC DRAINPIPE

DRAIN TO DRY WELL

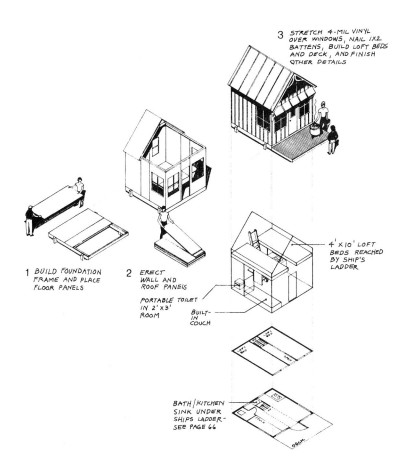

3 STRETCH 4-MIL VINYL
OVER WINDOWS, NAIL 1X2
BATTENS, BUILD LOFT BEDS
AND DECK, AND FINISH
OTHER DETAILS

1 BUILD FOUNDATION
FRAME AND PLACE
FLOOR PANELS

2 ERECT
WALL AND
ROOF PANELS

PORTABLE TOILET
IN 2'X3'
ROOM

BUILT-
IN
COUCH

4'X10' LOFT
BEDS REACHED
BY SHIP'S
LADDER

BATH/KITCHEN
SINK UNDER
SHIPS LADDER-
SEE PAGE 66

67

GEORGE BERNARD SHAW'S WRITING HUT

8′ × 8′
64 square feet

George Bernard Shaw, perhaps the most significant British playwright since the seventeenth century, wrote his most creative work, including his plays *Pygmalion*, *Heartbreak House*, *Back to Methuselah*, and *Saint Joan*, in a little writing hut at the bottom of his garden at his home in England.

Shaw designed the hut himself as a tiny office built on a central steel-pole frame so that it could be manually rotated to follow the arc of the sun. He worked alone and loved his privacy; he even adjusted his telephone for outgoing calls only.

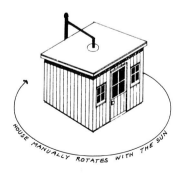

HOUSE MANUALLY ROTATES WITH THE SUN

ARCHITECT'S STUDIO

11'-6" × 11'-6"
132 square feet

On a beautiful wooded ledge, just far enough away from his house to make it a separate place, and just close enough to make it a short walk, architect David Minch has carefully crafted himself a tiny studio in the Adirondack Mountains style. The building is included here because it is both a comfortable workplace and because it exhibits such excellent craftsmanship. Because it is so small and because no one task is too large, the builder(s) can use extreme patience and care in its construction. David Minch learned woodworking by constructing a 40-foot Valiant 40 sailing yacht, taking three years of fourteen-hour work days to do so. His studio, built later and in a style totally distinct from that of his boat, exhibits the same profuse love of the craft of building.

One of the keys to the Adirondack Mountains style is the use of rough-cut boards with the bark left on one edge, as siding. This siding is known as Adirondack siding, or "flitch" siding (the untrimmed boards are known as "flitches").

The studio was designed around three large used fixed windows and two openable ones. David wanted the building to last for a very long time even though it might go untended, so he used flashing and caulking extensively and steeply sloped the windowsills.

The window detail shown in the photograph above illustrates the care given every detail of the construction. The flitch siding perfectly abuts the window trim, and the flashing line on the top trim piece is narrow and parallel.

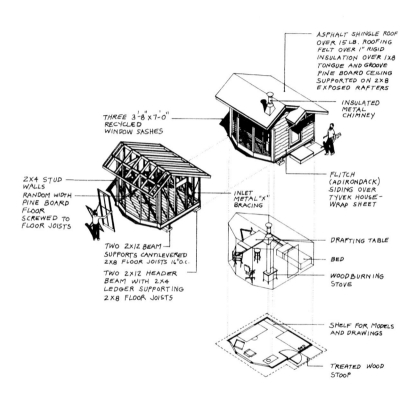

ASPHALT SHINGLE ROOF
OVER 15 LB. ROOFING
FELT OVER 1" RIGID
INSULATION OVER 1X8
TONGUE AND GROOVE
PINE BOARD CEILING
SUPPORTED ON 2X8
EXPOSED RAFTERS

INSULATED
METAL
CHIMNEY

THREE 3'-8" X 7'-0"
RECYCLED
WINDOW SASHES

FLITCH
(ADIRONDACK)
SIDING OVER
TYVEK HOUSE-
WRAP SHEET

2X4 STUD
WALLS
RANDOM WIDTH
PINE BOARD
FLOOR
SCREWED TO
FLOOR JOISTS

INLET
METAL "X"
BRACING

DRAFTING TABLE

BED

WOOD BURNING
STOVE

TWO 2X12 BEAM
SUPPORTS CANTILEVERED
2X8 FLOOR JOISTS 16"O.C.

TWO 2X12 HEADER
BEAM WITH 2X4
LEDGER SUPPORTING
2X8 FLOOR JOISTS

SHELF FOR MODELS
AND DRAWINGS

TREATED WOOD
STOOP

73

GUEST HOUSE

11' × 9'
99 square feet

This guest house was originally a tiny storage outbuilding, constructed in the same style and with the same materials as its adjacent main house and converted in 1978 by New York sculptor Anthony Krauss. It is special because of its size, just large enough for a bed, a desk, and some cooking facilities. The painted tin roof with cupola, and the rose arbor give the building a wonderfully cozy domestic character.

A renovation from a storage building to a guest house was accomplished primarily with a broom, paint, some furniture, and simple built-in painted pine and plywood shelves. The house will sleep one or two guests quite comfortably and also provide facilities for Mr. Krauss to use a quiet backyard retreat for his work.

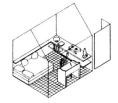

POETRY HOUSE

6' × 4'-4"
26 square feet

Carol Anthony is a gifted Connecticut artist whose best work is often conceived after a lengthy period of quietness, reading ot writing, in her humble Poetry House. "Solitude," she says, "is necessary nourishment for any creative process to begin."

Her Poetry House is an old weathered two-hole outhouse that she has beautifully, lovingly remodeled, with much help from her friend, furnituremaker Tommy Simpson, into a very pleasant little reading room. She calls it "a small, intimate slice of prose but representative of the bigger conversation of what I'm all about."

The history of Poetry House is a lesson in itself. This dilapidated, unused little outbuilding was given a new life—new use and an appropriate new rennovation with some elbow grease and poetic imagination.

The interior of Poetry House has a fresh coat of gloss white paint, two fixed glass windows at seat level, framed artwork, fresh-cut flowers, and just enough carpeting and pillows to accommodate a comfortable one- or two-hour reading session. Its shelves can hold as many books as needed, and a drink can be stored on an armrest between the two seats, now pillowed.

The exterior of Poetry House is weathered rough-cut pine boards and cedar shingles, cleverly embellished with wood carvings by Tommy Simpson. It sits on a 10′ × 10′ platform that gives the tiny building some stature and allows the interior, contemplative space to spill outside.

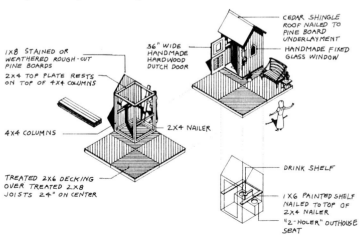

CEDAR SHINGLE ROOF NAILED TO PINE BOARD UNDERLAYMENT

36" WIDE HANDMADE HARDWOOD DUTCH DOOR

HANDMADE FIXED GLASS WINDOW

1×8 STAINED OR WEATHERED ROUGH-CUT PINE BOARDS

2×4 TOP PLATE RESTS ON TOP OF 4×4 COLUMNS

4×4 COLUMNS

2×4 NAILER

TREATED 2×6 DECKING OVER TREATED 2×8 JOISTS 24" ON CENTER

DRINK SHELF

1×6 PAINTED SHELF NAILED TO TOP OF 2×4 NAILER

"2-HOLER" OUTHOUSE SEAT

1950s RANCH HOUSE

12' × 9'
108 square feet

This classy little pink house with white trim sits just north of the Rappahannock River Bridge in a small development of tiny houses near Whitestone, Virginia. A 1960s Cadillac, completely dwarfing the house, is usually parked in the driveway.

Even though the house is tiny, it manages to exhibit most of the characteristics of a 1950s ranch house. On the exterior, first one sees the Cadillac, then the picture window, then the charcoal gray pyramidal roof and the pink clapboard siding, and on the interior, the drapes and the overstuffed furniture aimed at the TV. In fact, the lack of a dining table indicates that many TV dinners are probably consumed on the ever popular TV trays.

This house, or one like it, is a must project for nostagia buffs. Its platform frame construction on six concrete block foundation piers is a standard building procedure today. It would be very easy to build, and furnishing it would simply mean one exciting trip to the local used-furniture shop.

The primary materials of the ranch house are pink painted clap-boards, 1×4 white painted window and door trim, and a char-coal gray asphalt shingle roof over 2×4 rafters. All the windows and doors are standard types and sizes. This house requires, of course, a well, electricity, a kerosene stove, and an outhouse. The outhouse should be hidden because it is definitely not a 1950s item. The Cadillac is.

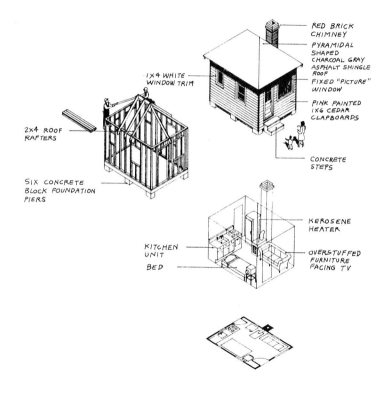

RED BRICK CHIMNEY

PYRAMIDAL SHAPED CHARCOAL GRAY ASPHALT SHINGLE ROOF

1X4 WHITE WINDOW TRIM

FIXED "PICTURE" WINDOW

PINK PAINTED 1X6 CEDAR CLAPBOARDS

2X4 ROOF RAFTERS

CONCRETE STEPS

SIX CONCRETE BLOCK FOUNDATION PIERS

KEROSENE HEATER

KITCHEN UNIT

OVERSTUFFED FURNITURE FACING TV

BED

83

FISHERMAN'S SHACK

16' × 12'
192 square feet

Wherever there is water there are fishermen's shacks, and often they can be converted into living quarters. This is especially true along the seacoast in the state of Maine. Tiny lobster fishing shacks abound Down East and are often available to anyone with enough time and imagination to convert a tiny 16' × 12' shed into a home.

The building shown here was a fisherman's shack until it was converted into a full-time residence in 1956 by a Lubec, Maine, woman. She lived there for nineteen years, raising two children and a host of pets. The tiny house had most modern conveniences except running water, which was hauled from a nearby spring. Television, washer/dryer, two types of cooking stoves, and living, dining, and sleeping areas for three all worked well. What was amazing was how all the furniture and appliances were arranged in the 192-square-foot space to accommodate movement and living patterns.

Fishermen's shacks are part of the New England vernacular style. They are outbuildings of Cape Cods, saltboxes, and coastal farmhouses built in the straightforward English colonial style of the early settlers. There are no roof overhangs because the strong winds, common along the northeast coast, would endanger the roof. Tiny windows were common because they lost less heat, and funny shack shapes developed because the buildings were continually added on to over a period of time.

The shack shown here was a 8' × 12' gable-roofed shed until it received an 8' × 12' saltbox addition sometime in the 1940s. Lace curtains and a TV antenna are inescapable signs of human habitation.

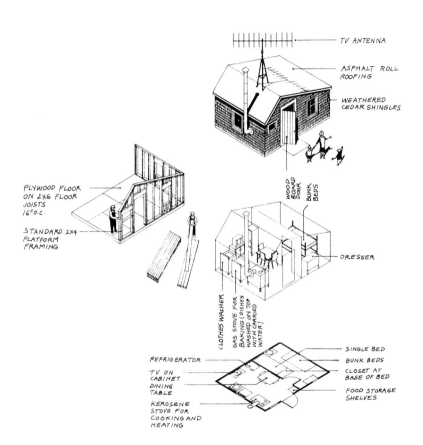

TV ANTENNA

ASPHALT ROLL ROOFING

WEATHERED CEDAR SHINGLES

PLYWOOD FLOOR ON 2X6 FLOOR JOISTS 16"O.C.

STANDARD 2X4 PLATFORM FRAMING

WOOD BOARD DOOR

BUNK BEDS

DRESSER

CLOTHES WASHER

GAS STOVE FOR BAKING (DISHES WASHED ON TOP WITH CARRIED WATER)

REFRIGERATOR

TV ON CABINET DINING TABLE

KEROSENE STOVE FOR COOKING AND HEATING

SINGLE BED

BUNK BEDS

CLOSET AT BASE OF BED

FOOD STORAGE SHELVES

87

DUNE SHACK

11' × 8'-6"
94 square feet

At the end of the nineteenth century, the United States Coast Guard patrolled the dangerous waters off Cape Cod near Provincetown by walking the beaches. In order to make their tour of duty more comfortable, they build tiny driftwood outbuildings in the dunes as quiet getaways from their bases. They also built a few to hold cows and hens and other domestic animals.

In the beginning of the 1900s some townspeople, anxious to spend more time on the desolate beaches and dunes, spent their summers constructing dune shacks of their own. By the 1920s a community of twenty to twenty-five tiny buildings existed along the dunes, back from the beaches, about an hour's walk from Provincetown. The shacks were inhabited then by naturalists, writers such as Eugene O'Neill, poets such as Harry Kemp, and artists. By the mid-1930's, the Coast Guard had left this part of the cape, and the Coast Guard station had slid into the sea. The shacks remained, lived in and maintained by the same inhabitants.

Today, about fifteen of these lovely weathered dune shacks still exist. The Cape Cod National Seashore of the United States Department of Interior is anxious to have them removed, but they are being challenged by the Peaked Hill Trust, a group of citizens who want to save the shacks.

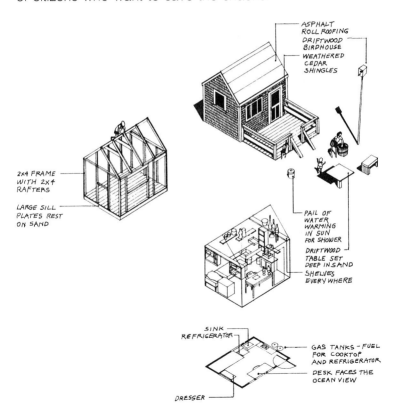

ASPHALT ROLL ROOFING

DRIFTWOOD BIRDHOUSE

WEATHERED CEDAR SHINGLES

2x4 FRAME WITH 2x4 RAFTERS

LARGE SILL PLATES REST ON SAND

PAIL OF WATER WARMING IN SUN FOR SHOWER

DRIFTWOOD TABLE SET DEEP IN SAND

SHELVES EVERYWHERE

SINK

REFRIGERATOR

GAS TANKS - FUEL FOR COOKTOP AND REFRIGERATOR

DESK FACES THE OCEAN VIEW

DRESSER

This dune shack is about 8 feet wide by 10 feet deep. A small potbelly stove is used for heating and cooking. It is a very special place, snuggled in between two small glassy dunes, facing the ocean. Everything, from the two sets of ''French'' doors (outside and screen) to the built-in bed in the back, is designed to take maximum advantage of the ocean view and prevailing summer breezes.

PHOTOGRAPHY CREDITS

The following people were immeasurably helpful and generous with their work:

Frontier Cabin
John Rice Irwin

Campground Cottage
Dukes County Historical Society

Sunday House
Gillespie County Historical Society

Earthquake Refugee Shack
Jim Kanne, Images West
Charles Stern, San Francisco History Collectors Association
San Francisco Archives

Rolling Home
Jane Lidz

Bolt-Together House
Jeff Milstein

Summer House

Jeff Milstein

Poetry House

Reprinted by permission from *House Beautiful*, copyright ©
November 1985, The Hearst Corporation. All rights reserved.
Photograph by William B. Seitz.

1950s Ranch House

David Minch

All other photographs were taken by the author.